for Nigel

A Chance of Love

sonnets of two decades

GW00702412

th best wishes

James Turner

James

Exeter Respect Festival 2022

Oversteps Books

First published in 2015 by   Oversteps Books Ltd
6 Halwell House
South Pool
Nr Kingsbridge
Devon
TQ7 2RX
UK

www.overstepsbooks.com

Printed in Great Britain by imprint digital, Devon

for Janet

The world is not different from us and our activities because it is what we are which creates the problems of the world.

J.Krishnamurti, *The First and Last Freedom*, Gollancz, 1954

Acknowledgements

These sonnets were written between 1992 and 2014. Some have been published before, often in earlier versions, in the following magazines and books:

Arvon Literary Intelligence, Envoi, Estuary: a Community Magazine for Topsham, The Frogmore Papers, Headlock, Iota, The Journal, Otter, Psychopoetica, Reflections, River King Poetry Supplement, Saw, Symmetry Pebbles (webzine); *Exeter Poetry Prize 1997: Anthology*, selected by Les Murray, Odyssey Press, 1997; *Forgeries*, by James Turner, Original Plus, 2002; *Listening to the Birth of Crystals: an Anthology to Benefit Deaf Children*, ed. Alan Corkish & Andrew Taylor, The People's Poet, 2003; *Creative Poetry Writing (Resource Books for Teachers* [series]), by Jane Spiro, Oxford University Press, 2004.

Personal Message to a Poetry Competition Judge won the Express & Echo Award in the Exeter Poetry Prize competition 1997. *Leaning Sonnet for Dominic Clare, Sculptor* was commissioned in 2006 by Dominic Clare for his website www.dominicclare.co.uk, where it stayed until around 2012, when the site was redesigned.

Last but not least, thanks to the following poetry venues, at one or other of which every one of these sonnets have been tried: One Night Stanza (Totnes), The Language Club (Plymouth), Poetry Island (Torquay), Taking the Mic (Exeter), Uncut Poets (Exeter).

Contents

Part 1: Work
Here 1
Owed to a Job 2
To a Crocus near my Workplace 3
Fear and Influence 4
I'm a Sonnet, John 5
Leaning Sonnet for Dominic Clare, Sculptor 6
This Fog 7
Lost in Translation 8
London, after Looking into Jung Chang's Wild Swans 9
To the Exe 10
Birth of a Poet 11
Always Already 12
Blessèd be the Postmodernists 13
Sonnet for a University Library Enquiry Desk 14
Personal Message to a Poetry Competition Judge 15
The End 16

Part 2: To be Vulnerable
Chat before Conception 17
Us and God 18
Time's Dupe 19
On Leave from Villa Two 20
In the Beginning 21
Life Sentence 22
Discipline 23
The Affair
 1. Love Poem 24
 2. Interrupted 25
 3. After 26
Generation 27
The Meaning of Life 28
One-Track 29
Portrait of the Artist 30
Reserve 31
Royal Wedding Sonnet 32

Sonnet to Me   33
Blue   34
The Vantage Point   35
Pavlov Sonnet 1   36
Pavlov Sonnet 2   37
Pavlov Sonnet 3   38
Pavlov Sonnet 4   39
Yehuda Amichai is Dead   40

Part 3: To be Nothing

Split   41
Postcard from Vague   42
Consider this Cat   43
This City   44
Freedom of Love   45
The Yellow Jug Inside   46
Autumn Wednesday   47
Personal   48
Clive's Question   49
Simplicity   50
Epitaph   51

Part 1. Work

*Each one must become aware of the issues of wrong
occupation with its disasters and miseries, weary routine
and death-dealing ways.*

J.Krishnamurti (conversation, Ojai, California, 9 July 1944)

Here

You like it here. Routine. Right angles, floor
and wall, those windows. Safe. The place to be,
return to, start from. Through that open door
and all along the path to work, you see
the tenements built up like syntax, hear
the sonnet's steady footfall marking time.
A breeze brings healing rain. And everywhere
the sweet familiarity of rhyme.

Away from this your clothes are wrong. It's cold.
You set out early, yet you turn up late.
You can't buy shoes to fit your blistered feet.
The people speak of people you don't know.
At every turn you learn the rules have changed.
Nothing adds up. No poem is complete.

Owed to a Job

I guess I'm hooked. I need you to keep sane.
You give me sunshine mornings saved from sleep,
distraction, shelter from the cold and rain,
money (although my labour's rather cheap),
motive, meaning, a structure and some friends.
You irrigate the wastes of vacant time
so tea-breaks flower, and evenings, and weekends
(by Thursday thoughts of Sunday seem sublime).
And you're a phrase to fill in forms with, speak
in answer to the question 'What d'you do?'
A drug to drown the fear of being unique.
A link with normal life. The strangest glue.
In twenty years I've learnt two things about you.
You bore me stiff. And I'd be stuck without you.

To a Crocus near my Workplace

Somewhere there's a brighter crocus, surely,
busting open under taller trees,
a spot to view the distant hills more clearly,
a place of higher learning, whose degrees
count for more in a better ordered world
where truth is given more respect than lies,
where spring comes sooner, more leaves have uncurled
and birds are courting under bluer skies —
a campus where the library employs
a keener class of library assistant
to issue books, charge fines and keep down noise,
more of whom are morally resistant
to crimes like wasting time, though one mean man
can write far slicker sonnets than I can.

Fear and Influence

Halfway to work this morning I met John.
We walked a yard or two together. I
was late and hurrying, and John said, *Why*
this most unseemly haste? What's going on?
I looked at him and thought. The sun shone.
He was just as late and in no hurry.
I saw the point. I said, *Why should we worry?*
How old's the human race d'you reckon, one,
two million years? If after all that time
we're scared of being a minute late .... I slowed.
Bit of perspective, eh? said John. *Indeed!*
What's lateness after all? I said. *A crime?*
Then John turned left down Pennsylvania Road.
I sauntered on a while — then picked up speed.

I'm a Sonnet, John

You've seen my type before a hundred times,
and though we go back centuries, still you find
we treat our subjects special, safe behind
walls five feet thick and windows barred with rhymes.
Last time you met my author — late last June,
remember? — former workmate James, you know 'im —
Why don't you put me in a bleedin' poem?
you asked him. Talk about a change of tune!
John, you're a worldly man. Surely you knew
the price of preservation, how you'd live,
the sentences to run consecutive.
You scratch your stubble-chin. What's wrong with you?
You looking for the door? There isn't one.
You're written down. You're here for ever, John.

Leaning Sonnet for Dominic Clare, Sculptor

Head carved from a telegraph pole, grain circles
around the eyes. Elm bur bowl. Ash stool.
Vessel in polished halves stitched together
with rope, for carrying air. Slatted head
with gentle Ethiopian lips: walk past
and see it crescendo benign to so intense
it almost scares. Recycled bicycle
a freewheel lesson in how to be yourself
no striving after. Pale rough-wood tower, with holes
burnt chimney-black by brushwood fire ignited
by sparks from a sculptor's eye. Wood spirals up
buzzard-on-a-thermal all chainsaw-glide
no flap. Enough to start a hundred poets
chiselling sonnets out of writer's block.

Not mentioned in this poem is Clare's "Leaning Tower" (2004).

This Fog

It's like there was this fog, you see, or rather,
don't see, don't even see the fog, and yet
out of it words come. Feed some back and if
you're lucky it responds with further words.
Fog? It's too thick for fog! It's porridge rather,
familiar sludge. It's everywhere and yet
nowhere. It soothes *and* hurts. If flows, but if
pushed it will tense, which deafens it to words.
When you're morose it's all there is, no hint
of light, just liquid mud, the viscous pull of it,
and no way in and no way out. But when
a distant source transmits, it picks up int-
ermittent signals. Fizz! You're happy then.
A radio made of mud, your head's full of it.

Lost in Translation

meditation on a remark by Les Murray

Chinese poems are nothing like *The Sun*,
The Daily Mirror, Times or *Guardian*, yet their
translators multiply their words to get their
drift or they'd sound like headlines. (GOTCHA! FUN
RUN ENDS IN BLOOD BATH. GIANT GRABS AT CRUMBS.)
A bit like History, whose sieve retains
just diagram bones while detail-dapple drains
away to dark. All leaf, all flesh succumbs.

I have a nightmare. I'm being sucked by Time
down History's anticlockwise plughole, drowned
for being sole witness to the world's worst crime.
Meanwhile the bones of my unfinished book
are ground to dust and then washed underground
to join the thick-polluted stream Shitbrook.

*Shitbrook was the stream that flowed just south of Exeter's city wall and
into the River Exe. After the cholera outbreak of 1832 it went underground
as the Barnfield Brook Sewer.*

London, after Looking into Jung Chang's Wild Swans

To fathom the workings of a Western town,
go and lean over Lambeth Bridge and breathe
London in, while an August sun beats down
and pleated muddy waters slide beneath.
Not as a social historian or scholar
of any kind, nor as a painter, poet,
journalist or Mr Average Fella,
but as a Chinese immigrant I'd know it.
For him each busker, each train that runs on time,
each office block exudes significance;
from Soho to the City, in open collusion,
the people work the systems, even crime
holds meaning, and the homeless join the dance.
The antidote to Cultural Revolution.

To the Exe

Dallier, dasher, mallard-bearer, cloud-
and sun- and moon-reflector, irrigator,
drowner, divider, bridge-necessitator —
don't you think a poet should be allowed,
encouraged even, to speak of you as you,
not as mere metaphor for life's mad journey?
Your depths are brown, your banks are grassed or ferny,
your silt is soft, and flow is what you do,
you dirty flooder — old, but not old man —
through Time, it's true, but chiefly past me, south
through woods and fields and city, moor to mouth.
Your boats are boats: you sink them when you can.
Your fish are fish and caught with hooks and nets.
Your Topsham avocets are avocets.

Birth of a Poet

You never liked the poems I really *meant*,
that spoke the things I felt, in my own voice.
"But all's not lost", you said. "You're spoilt for choice
in fact. Invention's power is never spent:
invent that you still have it, that's the trick.
Ready? Write down the scene in front of you.
Insert a stolen paragraph or two.
Cut up the page. Shuffle the pieces. Stick
them back together. Like this, see?" I saw.
Chopped phrases sprang to life as sound-effects,
a catch-breath crunch of splintered metaphor.
"Now read it out", you said. "More will appear.
The sense has vanished, yet the brain connects."
"You mean —" I stopped. And started my career.

Always Already

The real is not only what can be reproduced, but that which is always already reproduced.

Jean Baudrillard, early postmodern philosopher

You started out a seeker after fact,
believed that what you are is what you know,
believed that gaining knowledge makes you grow,
a storage place the only thing you lacked.
Hope was, all through your youth, that you could do it:
read books, accumulate some truth,
so ignorance, the fault that goes with youth,
would be gone by the time you'd struggled through it.

It stayed. And time went by. And now you're old
you see the book you're reading page by page
dissolve into the ignorance of age.
On brittle branches no fresh leaves unfold.
Longing for new air, rarified and heady,
all you ever breathe is *always already*.

Blessèd be the Postmodernists

Go on, enjoy. Have jolly surrealist fun.
Play language games. Campaign fiercely against
closure and the consecutive. Go on
getting smarter. Refuse to be entranced
by the rough granite of the deeply felt.
Gather ye plenteous blooms, both live and plastic,
into one massive bouquet of contempt,
binding the slender stems with *truth's elastic*.
Never allow, *beyond your own idea of it,*
the thing itself, an *other*. Go on constructing
worlds from bits of world. Make a career of it,
teach it, sell it, watch your takings mount.
Ignore our protest-groans, we're only acting.
Please don't disturb yourselves on our account.

Sonnet for a University Library Enquiry Desk

Sorry, can't help, I'm meant symbolically.
Don't ask what kind of truth lurks in this line,
that phrase, this trope, that praise, this long-drawn whine.
Music and meaning, these make poetry,
not truth. Suppose I list the things I see.
Professor. Carpet. Swing doors. Exit sign.
The I whose eye beholds them might be mine
or might belong to some fictitious me.
The objects in my list may not be there,
in which case you would say I was a liar —
if this were not a poem. Is it? Oh,
not much of one, it's true. What? You don't care
about the truth, you're after something higher?
You could be fiction too, for all I know.

Personal Message to a Poetry Competition Judge

Now for the poet, he nothing affirmeth, and therefore never lieth.

Philip Sidney

Hi Judge, it's me. My surname rhymes with learner.
I'm on a learning curve. I want to be
a forger, see. This poem's a forgery.
Are you a fake as well, or True Discerner?
Surely a Judge should seem a whole lot sterner.
This ain't a Poem anyhow, or we
should redefine the concept 'Poetry'.
I'd love to be a Judge — nice little earner —
but I'm no poet. That stuff's all innate.
I always lacked it, even in my youth.
Its language I have never understood
and never will. I do not deprecate
myself, I speak the truth. I speak the truth,
and not some damned Persona. Got that? Good.

This poem was entered for a competition judged by Les Murray.

The End

It seemed an average day. We'd had no warning.
Outside the drizzle was composed of water.
Inside, *I'm two towels short again this morning,*
I heard the cleaning lady tell the porter.
In Audiovisual, daffodils — stiff stars,
proud as when they were picked five years before —
still glowed dim air-dried yellow in their vase
as the air-conditioning hummed. On the ground floor
the desk-staff, bored and lacking a queue, were shirking.
They Googled, or tapped emails to their friends,
knowing they'd still get wages minus taxes.
Books gathered dust. The staff lift wasn't working.
With barely a wobble in its current trends,
the earth continued spinning on its axis.

Part 2. To be Vulnerable

To be vulnerable is to live, to withdraw is to die.
J. Krishnamurti, *Commentaries on Living: Second Series,*
edited by D. Rajagopal, Gollancz, 1959

Chat before Conception

Want to be born? What, me? *Yes, you.* Some question!
Well, do you? Now's your chance. How should I know?
Pearl-grey for ever here. And if I go?
There's colour. Hunger, food — And indigestion?
There's grief as well as joy. Will I be wise?
Unlikely, but — A chance of love, or not?
A chance. If I can't stand the pain, then what?
There's always death. Mmm. What would you advise?
The whole thing's up to you. I'm interested.
The start's the tricky part. Dependency?
Correct. You mean you cannot guarantee
two decent parents? *Right.* And when I'm dead?
No second chance. All right — I'll go. No, wait!
I've one more question — *Sorry, friend. Too late.*

Us and God

Suppose there is one God, as some maintain.
Further suppose that God created us,
all life from artichoke to octopus;
the earth, its moon-tide oceans, sun and rain;
the galaxies and everything between.
What kind of God did that? Amazing, clever —
to get it started, keep it going, whatever.
Incredible, all-powerful King — or Queen?

I'd say He's male. I'll tell you why. It's not
because He's boss of the entire caboodle
(a female boss could manage just as well),
it's His mistakes. Just look at us, at what
we suffer. Only a male designer's doodle
could lead to such a *careless* kind of hell.

Time's Dupe

Whatever happened to the present tense?
Till you became time's dupe, it loved you well,
but where you once felt safe is now a hell,
a ceaseless march, a clockwork of events.
Back then you knew just where you were
and understood without attending classes.
Today, through your best pair of mental glasses,
nothing comes into focus but a blur.
Until it disappeared behind a hedge,
you thought it would outlast you, all that Now,
that chewing on the moment like a cow.
Now, hanging by your fingers from a ledge
high above siren, horn and engine-hum,
you feel your fingers weaken and grow numb.

On Leave from Villa Two

I'll miss one weekly parley with the shrink.
Ten minutes. Well, to talk with him much longer
would only make him nervous, late, or think,
or, worse for me, prescribe me something stronger.

A week off ritual humiliation
by Trivial Pursuit. Well, ignorance
is all I know, though sunken information
has struggled up through deep mud more than once.

On leave (but still on psychoactive tether),
as if doing endless jigsaws weren't just play
but service, hard, like being in the army.
Well, jigsaws draw a few of us together
in gentle mental discipline each day.
But *leave*? From *this*? I guess they think we're barmy.

In the Beginning

In the beginning there was fire, and all
the multiverse of truth, and to belong
was all. In the beginning was the fall.
Right from the start a sense of something wrong,
which those around affected not to feel,
smothered your flame, stopped up its whispered song,
distorted your perception of the real.
Your hands were bound, you choked on acrid smoke,
while world on world was closed with doors of steel.
Did no one near you see it? No one spoke,
and no one held your hand or heard you groan,
though ocean shrank to droplets as you woke,
and sky to splintered glass, and time to bone.
Was I not with you then? You weren't alone.

Life Sentence

Time on time through geologic layers
this life evolved a game of chance whose players
all innocent risked all for life, competed
for food but lived for love, died undefeated
while all creation flowed in spontaneity,
faded to flower in chance and pain and gaiety
and time was simply sequence night and day
and brains were much too small to block the way
till evolution threw up thought and hands,
misspelt the ends of all creation's plans,
for thought conspired with hand in perfect crime
to bind the tender infant chance with time
so children grow in fear and greed and sadness
to hand them on not grasping this is madness.

Discipline

When he taught you obedience as a child
it was in part: do as the grownups tell you,
be good, not bad, be civilised, not wild,
however much the idea might repel you.
And in part it was: he believed sincerely
that if he didn't show you he was boss
you'd run amuck — that you were evil, really,
and he must make you good by getting cross.

But there was something else, a thing so wrong
that nobody, not even you, must know.
And yet in part you knew it all along,
unconsciously of course, but it would show.
An absent look. A tendency to blush.
An awkwardness not even he could crush.

The Affair

1. Love Poem

I worked all week, lived quietly alone,
on Saturdays I'd shop, on Sundays migraine,
a gentle walk most evenings. That's all gone,
a state of grace I'll never know again.
With winds that gust to gale force in exposed
places driving me everywhere at once, it's
scary. I don't know how — a bend in the road,
a change of gear — things just took off. Concerts,
readings, workshops, meetings, late nights chatting —
my diary's full, an endless manic phase.
No time for anything — too much to do.
My single room's a dustbin. Keep forgetting
where I've put what, and why. Coping? Was.
Till Wednesday. Just. Then Thursday I met you.

2. Interrupted

What knob was turned, what button pressed? What flap
flipped over by what hidden force allowed
what non-stop stream to flow? What broke the cloud,
letting a shaft of what shine through the gap?
D'you think all this adds up to love? If so,
I never asked for it and nor did you.
It thrills but doesn't tell me what to do.
Go out and buy a pack of condoms. No.
Yes. No. Its fiery logic shifts too fast,
showing up every line of thought as flawed.
Not long ago the worst I felt was bored.
How long does this new brand of madness last?
Let's douse it now, before we're both consumed.
Let normal humdrum service be resumed.

3. After

She says that she feels used. I say, *But how?*
Wasn't it mutual, the thing we had?
Oh, it was mutual once, she says, *but now ...*
She means I've changed the past, I've turned it bad.
By saying our partnership has ceased to work,
I've smudged for her the colour of each kiss
long after it has dried, I've soured each look
and loving word *in retrospect.* Unless
I staged what I believe was from the heart,
my few small gifts just bribes, my smiles all fake.
Or we were dreaming, and are now awake —
when we seemed one, we were in fact apart.
But while the magic worked, who cast the spell?
If I tricked her, I tricked myself as well.

Generation

I come from where red houses multiplied,
wild daffodils gave way to gaudier blooms,
and on the walls of inward-looking rooms
hung paintings of a vanished countryside.
I come from where red houses stood correct
and square and built to last. And still they stand.
My father's father was the builder and
my mother's father was the architect.

From time to time I go back in my head
and there, age 5, I'm present at a birth:
our black cat having kittens on my bed.
I run to tell my mother, overjoyed
that such a thing could happen on this earth,
and can't imagine why she's so annoyed.

The Meaning of Life

is when you overhear yourself say yes
knowing no is better, it's when, when a person
asks you *How old am I?*, you pitch your guess
ten years too high, it's when you fall to cursing
someone a new friend you're conversing with
admires, it's when unthinkingly you speak
political offence, it's when you give
a blameless aunt a book about some freak,
murderess, thief or prostitute whose name
you suddenly remember is the same
as hers, it's when you carelessly allow
swing doors to swing at someone right behind you,
it's when you want to press *delete* but know
no matter where you run or hide they'll find you.

One-Track

I met a teacher back in the late 60s
who asked me what I did. *I'm unemployed,*
I said. He paused a while in thought, then fixed his
protruding eyes on me, assured, devoid
of condescension. *When d'you think you're winning?*
he asked. My turn to pause. "When I'm out walking,"
I said. Not now, a party just beginning,
I didn't add. Two men, not given to talking,
trapped in this dimly-lit suburban flat,
students and teachers socialising round us.
I didn't learn, he didn't try to teach,
so no one won or lost. And that was that —
except some grim unvoiced agreement bound us,
two one-track minds, beyond each other's reach.

Portrait of the Artist

I stand before you incomplete, my friends,
my absent bits kept back by hidden laws.
Still, I can speak to you — some let-out clause
has let me out to navigate the bends,
unpick the tangled strands and make amends.
I thank you for your welcoming applause
but I can't tell my story yet because
I don't know how it starts or how it ends.
Suppose instead I gather up some pieces
of it, clean them, iron out the creases,
then glue them onto canvas — would you call
that art? Or drop them into molten glass,
then pour that into oblong moulds — they'd pass
as sculpture, no? Enough to build a wall.

Reserve

I caught her eye (I don't know who smiled first),
then turned my back to take a window seat
not far from hers, and when the train moved off
I thought until I thought my brain might burst
of her, her eyes, how fresh she looked, how neat
her page-boy hair, and listened to her cough.
What if I'd sat beside her, tried to speak?
That needed an excuse (I couldn't see one)
or I'd have disconcerted her I thought,
afraid she'd be afraid I was a freak.
But if that seat had been the only free one ...
Such conflict calls for coffee, so, distraught,
I struggle to my feet — then turn to look.
Her head's bent over, eyes down on her book.

Returning from the buffet car, I see
she's staring through the window, book on lap.
I pause a second (she won't look at me),
resume my seat. The train soon starts to slow,
jerking the family opposite from nap
to panic: their stop next, not long to go
and shoes to be put on, bags on the floor,
and on the table toys and flask and cup
and scattered food wait to be gathered up.
The train stops, and off down the corridor
they trip, except the elder son who stays
to pack the last few things then follow fast.
He leaves one bag behind. Inert, I gaze ...
it's not too late ... but now the moment's passed.

The page-boy girl runs after him with it.
I sit and think. I wish I could just sit.

Royal Wedding Sonnet

for Helen

I didn't know there was a royal wedding
next weekend, I confess. *What* do *you mean?*
she asks, incredulous. *I mean …*   I'm treading
gingerly. I might well have heard or seen
news of it somewhere, but the recent past's
a misty glass to me. *There's other ways*
of putting it, I add (like: Nothing lasts
for long in my world, when they're done my days
drop through a hole to nothingness, I'd keep
a notebook in my head to make them stay
but that falls too, I'm scared the rot is spreading
and daily dread dementia's stealthy sleep,
its death-in-life), *but simpler just to say*
I didn't know there was a royal wedding.

Sonnet to Me

Le Cygne by Saint-Saëns on trombone
instead of 'cello. Brambles taking hold,
blood on your finger, taste of salt. The 'phone —
it's not for you. You're fifty-one years old,
you should know better. That's a north wind blowing.
The skies are clear at night for comet-viewing
and hazy blue by day. Your memory's going.
You're doing it quite a lot these days — chewing
your tongue. You hate it when Clare mentions it.
The trees are coming into leaf like. Day
by day in every way.* You try to fit
a word between two other words. It won't.
Poetry. That's the latest news you say.
Your tongue — you're chewing it again James. Don't.

* *These two truncated quotations are from* The Trees, *in* The Whitsun Weddings *by Philip Larkin* (The trees are coming into leaf/Like something almost being said), *and from Emile Coué's own preferred translation of his once-famous formula for health by autosuggestion* (Day by day, in every way, I'm getting better and better).

Blue

I love *that blue!* you sigh, then smile, then laugh
the clouds apart. Can one love blue that much?
I'm not averse to it myself, but ... such
passion! A colour for your other half!
The joy that bubbled up when blue was new —
that can't still flow! Oh, I could understand
your words as hope, as impotent command,
as showing off, or simply as untrue,
for keeping up a front is not a crime
but tact, or tactic: everyone pretends,
or loses credibility and friends
(well nobody is honest all the time).
A lie I might forgive, or any sin,
but this affair with blue is genuine.

The Vantage Point

Dad, from the vantage point of your deathbed,
can you see further? Tell me, are we merely
the sum of all our sins, the books we've read,
the clothes we've worn, the tunes we've whistled? Really
what is a man? Must I wait till I'm nearly
a corpse myself, all blue-veined white, before
I find out too? Or can't you see so clearly
what all we folk with futures so ignore?

Your blank stare tells me it's too late to ask.
Dad, it's a wonder you survived the op!
Behind your face behind the oxygen mask,
bulldozed chunk by chunk into the pit,
the memories roll and drop, roll and drop.
The last one drops, and then ... I guess that's it.

Pavlov Sonnet 1

... the representative of the animal kingdom which is man's best friend.
I. P. Pavlov, Nobel Prize Address, Stockholm, 1904

I give you Ivan Petrovich Pavlov!
Let's be upstanding, raise our glasses, quaff,
and meditate upon this man's renown
as fiery gulps of vodka filter down,
via oesophagus, to digestive tract,
a place where Pavlov sought his 'Mr Fact' —
but not in human subjects: he chose dogs
to help dispel Count Fiction's mental fogs.
Hard science would banish war and discontent
with hard fact gleaned from dog-experiment,
and if his methods made dogs howl and squeal,
hard luck, it was mankind he aimed to heal.
But what's mankind if serving it can end
in sacrificing dog, mankind's best friend?

Man, mankind — *this was the language of Pavlov, his translators and his
times. Indeed, it was mostly men who, in the name of male-dominated
science, and in order to serve a male-dominated humanity, committed the
cruelties alluded to in these poems.*

Pavlov Sonnet 2

For science to probe the workings of the world
effectively, it must be given leave
to bugger it about. We must believe
that lifeless matter feels no pain when hurled
against itself, nor deems itself degraded
when peered at upside-down or inside-out,
for matter has no rights to speak about
or any privacy to be invaded.
And so the mill grinds on, and there's no stopping it.
But living tissue too is science's food.
In recent years we've heard of scientists copping it
for slicing into living flesh and brains.
If Pavlov's fingers, stained with canine blood,
won him that Prize, that Prize, too, bears the stains.

Pavlov Sonnet 3

We Humans have to do things other creatures
don't, like converse, and plan, and put up shelves.
Yet Pavlov held that studying them can teach us
a lot about our much more complex selves.
All creatures are machines, at least in part
(he'd read the book *Reflexes of the Brain*
by Sechenov, and taken it to heart).
And he saw science as more than just explain.
As Newton split white beams of light with prisms
to recombine their colours into white,
so Pavlov would reveal mind's mechanisms
one at a time (to isolate that blight
that causes misery and war, his goal),
to map the whole machine, then *take control.*

Pavlov Sonnet 4

In days gone by they told us everlasting hell
would punish those who died as unrepentant sinners —
they feared that nothing less would be enough to quell
an ever-present tendency to evil in us —
and furthermore they told us everlasting bliss
rewarded all who died repentant-faithful-good.
They reckoned most of us, believing all of this,
would at the very least sin less (of course we would! —
how stupid did they think we were?), but just in case,
our prudent legislators also put in place
rod, thumbscrew, gallows, fire and other retributions,
to keep their hierarchies safe from revolutions
and stop us looting churches, should hell lose its sting.
I.P. Pavlov didn't invent conditioning.

Yehuda Amichai is Dead

The unofficial laureate who described
private life in a land where war is normal.
Then what of dear old England? What of us,
from childhood scorned/indulged and threatened/bribed,
a boiling mass of contradictions, formal/
informal, come on, make/don't make a fuss,
public/private, amenable/resistant?
No shells explode here, yet we're not at peace:
our soldiers fight abroad. Our wars are distant,
our streets defended by the ultimate bomb,
but also intimate. We never cease
to fight our inward Battles of the Somme,
and win, and therefore lose. All red is blood:
no poppies on this victory's sterile mud.

Yehuda Amichai, poet, born Germany 1924, died Jerusalem, 22nd Sept.
2000. The quotation is from his obituary in the Times.

Part 3. To be Nothing

... to be nothing, completely nothing, then in that state there is compassion.
J.Krishnamurti, *The Book of Life*, HarperCollins, 1975

Split

A single body houses two men,
or two selves rather, one the dreamer,
passive, naïve, and one the schemer,
controller, thinker. Both are human —
and here's the substance of this sermon —
both are essential. We in the West
tend to assume the thinker's best
at knowing what's best. That clever German
Marx was a prime example. Nietzsche,
though, was a rarer kind of teacher
who could acknowledge, even respect it,
the hectored half, that hard-whipped horse —
could hear its shrieks and weep. (Of course
he went on whipping till he'd wrecked it.)

Postcard from Vague

Hillview Hotel. Dear mum and dad, which hill
it was where Vague's first settler saw his Vision
nobody knows with any great precision,
or if it was some mind-contracting pill
he'd popped, or brain damage, if he was ill
with fever, mad, or what. But much derision
was heaped on him at first, then came the prison
of psychiatric ward, and yet his will,
though bent, remained unbroken. Weather chillier
here, and it's always hazy. Food quite good.
The people all seem vaguely unfamiliar
but friendly. I feel un-misunderstood
for once — you know, when laughter meets with laughter.
I'm back next week. Or maybe the week after.

Consider this Cat

Comparison denies the essence of
the person being compared. Like this. I feel
inadequate. Asked why, I say I'd love
to have that man's ability to reel
off facts and figures, this man's sense of humour,
that man's sexual prowess, this man's skill
in juggling five cheese rolls with one satsuma
balancing on his chin. But we can't *will*
the way we want to be. The truth is *this*
and what we think we've got to be is *that*.
This unambitious cat is just a cat
yet lives in undivided consciousness.
He's got the thing we're after, there's no doubt,
yet we who have the brains can't work it out.

This City

I love this city. Why, God only knows.
Twenty-five years I've lived here, long enough
for it and me to forge a bond I suppose.
A chemistry of street and heart. That stuff.

You say I'm sick, I say the sick love most.
Even the bus-station café doesn't depress me,
where I quite often come for tea and toast,
though when I don't they don't complain they miss me.

At the next table a little girl has squeezed
one teabag dry and shoved another inside
her mouth. Mum beckons her, not too displeased —
she knows true clowns are hard to discipline —
but the girl keeps out of reach, eyes laughing-wide,
two dark brown tea-drops trickling down her chin.

Freedom of Love

after Dean Atta after André Breton

My mother who knew what was proper and never swore
                                  worse than *damn*,
who drove a Rover and never had to worry about money,
who could laugh until the tears came at absurd or merely funny,
who gardened, knitted jumpers, and made cushions and jam —
my mother who was steadily there for her children when needed,
who worried about us a lot but didn't interfere
when we suffered in love, or mental or physical health, or career,
but always rejoiced with us when we revived or succeeded —
my mother who didn't just tell us but showed us right and good,
who loved people whatever their station and helped them
                                  when she could,
who kept her clothes and house and friendships in good repair —
my mother who was mostly cheerful and mostly well,
but whose last nine weeks of life were post-op hospital hell,
stayed free, right to the end, of self-pity and despair.

The Yellow Jug Inside

A city with no yellow jug inside it
isn't a city. Our jug glows through glaze
cracked like a spider's web or street-map maze
and a hundred thousand hearts combine to hide it.
Crossing a street we cradle it with care.
Descending steps or threading through a crowd,
sheer magic to us just to be allowed
to lug this yellow jug round everywhere.
Symbol perhaps, but what it means we simply
won't spell out, or can't, and that's because
to us it's just a jug, all surface flaws,
no handle, cracked, misshapen, chipped and pimply.
Design the city logo round it? God, no.
It's our secret. Don't let every sod know.

Autumn Wednesday

I'm older than I've ever been before.
As each day dawns I'm older by a day.
The grub that gobbled Tuesday's wanting more.
Its name is time, and time is here to stay.

Its chomping started back when I did. Then
it scared the child I was, and made him ill,
though once or twice before the age of ten
it stopped, a glimpse of calm that haunts me still.

Time's not a problem these days anyhow,
its speed cannot be slowed, and I don't try,
for now will always go on being now
though day may follow day until I die.
That falling leaf. Those unseen running feet.
The soft light on that roof across the street.

Personal

I'm tired of all your news and gossip. Tell me rather
how many different human emotions are there?
Spare me your real-life soap and all that lather,
fish only emotions from the headlong flow,
extract the true transparent from the cloudy sham in them,
stop them, freeze them there, and let me examine them
as I could only dream of while I swam in them,
arranged upon a table in a row.
The shame that makes for loneliness, which I mistook
for personal, so personal no book
would have it, not even Kafka — I could look
along the row and find it small and naked there,
stripped of narrative self, and I might dare
stare back for once at its unholy stare.

Clive's Question

Who are *you?* Clive at the Victory Centre wonders.
He knows my occupation, age and name.
Nudging his clients onward, that's his game,
to places that till now have seemed beyond us.
I walk out from the Centre on a high
which doesn't last — no good mood ever does —
but something silent lying behind the buzz
survives, and lifting fog reveals that I

am *nothing*. Empty space. An open door
through which you might observe this fuddled man,
and the same self that spoke through him before
Clive's question, doing its level best to hide him
by faking a certain feverish élan,
now lets some air play round the wounds inside him.

Simplicity

Wherever here, whenever now may be,
where he is now's the testing ground for all
suggestion, guess, belief, philosophy.
However loud the past and elsewhere call,
where he is now is any human mind,
its hand, its eye and ear, its nose and tongue.
Beyond the hope ahead, the fear behind,
that sky, these streets, the folk he moves among —
are only images and information
and news and lies and news and nothing else.
One memory holds the history of the race,
one crocus in the grass is all creation,
all sound is in one distant peal of bells
and every woman's kindness in one face.

Epitaph

One night he dreamt that he let go the raft,
fashioned from knobbly logs of memory
lashed together with vain hopes fore and aft,
that kept him buoyed upon this queasy sea —

he dreamt of letting go and sinking, faster,
deeper, far into unplumbed mystery smooth
and cool as milk, empty as hunger, vaster
than a cathedral, elusive as the truth —

woke with a start, still clinging on somehow.
Years passed, till finally the clumsy bloke
he was let go for real. Where is he now?

Posterity must flounder on without him —
his raft and body both went up in smoke.
There's nothing more I want to say about him.

Oversteps Books Ltd

The Oversteps list includes books by the following poets:

David Grubb, Giles Goodland, Alex Smith, Will Daunt, Patricia Bishop, Christopher Cook, Jan Farquarson, Charles Hadfield, Mandy Pannett, Doris Hulme, James Cole, Helen Kitson, Bill Headdon, Avril Bruton, Marianne Larsen, Anne Lewis-Smith, Mary Maher, Genista Lewes, Miriam Darlington, Anne Born, Glen Phillips, Rebecca Gethin, W H Petty, Melanie Penycate, Andrew Nightingale, Caroline Carver, John Stuart, Rose Cook, Jenny Hope, Hilary Elfick, Jennie Osborne, Anne Stewart, Oz Hardwick, Angela Stoner, Terry Gifford, Michael Swan, Denise Bennett, Maggie Butt, Anthony Watts, Joan McGavin, Robert Stein, Graham High, Ross Cogan, Ann Kelley, A C Clarke, Diane Tang, Susan Taylor, R V Bailey, John Daniel, Alwyn Marriage, Simon Williams, Kathleen Kummer, Jean Atkin, Charles Bennett, Elisabeth Rowe, Marie Marshall, Ken Head, Robert Cole, Cora Greenhill, John Torrance, Michael Bayley, Christopher North, Simon Richey, Lynn Roberts, Sue Davies, Mark Totterdell, Michael Thomas, Ann Segrave, Helen Overell and Rose Flint.

For details of all these books, information about Oversteps and up-to-date news, please look at our website and blog:

www.overstepsbooks.com
http://overstepsbooks.wordpress.com